INDIANS OF AMERICA

Pontiac
INDIAN GENERAL AND STATESMAN

MATTHEW G. GRANT

Illustrated by Harold Henriksen

GALLERY OF GREAT AMERICANS SERIES

Pontiac
INDIAN GENERAL AND STATESMAN

Text copyright © 1974 by Publications Associates. Illustrations copyright © 1974 by Creative Education. International copyrights reserved in all countries. No part of this book may be reproduced in any form without written permission from the publisher. Printed in the United States.

Library of Congress Number: 73-12193

ISBN: 0-87191-268-6

Published by Creative Education, Mankato, Minnesota 56001

Library of Congress Cataloging in Publication Data
Grant, Matthew G
    Pontiac, Indian general and statesman.
    (His Indians of America) (Gallery of great Americans series)
    SUMMARY: A biography of the Ottawa war chief whose almost successful plan to join many tribes together to defeat the British was known as Pontiac's Conspiracy.
    1. Pontiac, Ottawa chief, d. 1769—Juvenile literature. 1. Pontiac, Ottawa chief, d. 1769. 2. Ottawa Indians—Biography. 3. Indians of North America—Biography. I. Henriksen, Harold, illus. II. Title. E83.76.P2G72 970.3 B 92 73-12193 ISBN 0-87191-268-6

CONTENTS

THE GREAT LAKES INDIANS	7
PONTIAC'S CONSPIRACY	13
THE PONTIAC WAR BEGINS	19
THE UPRISING FAILS	27

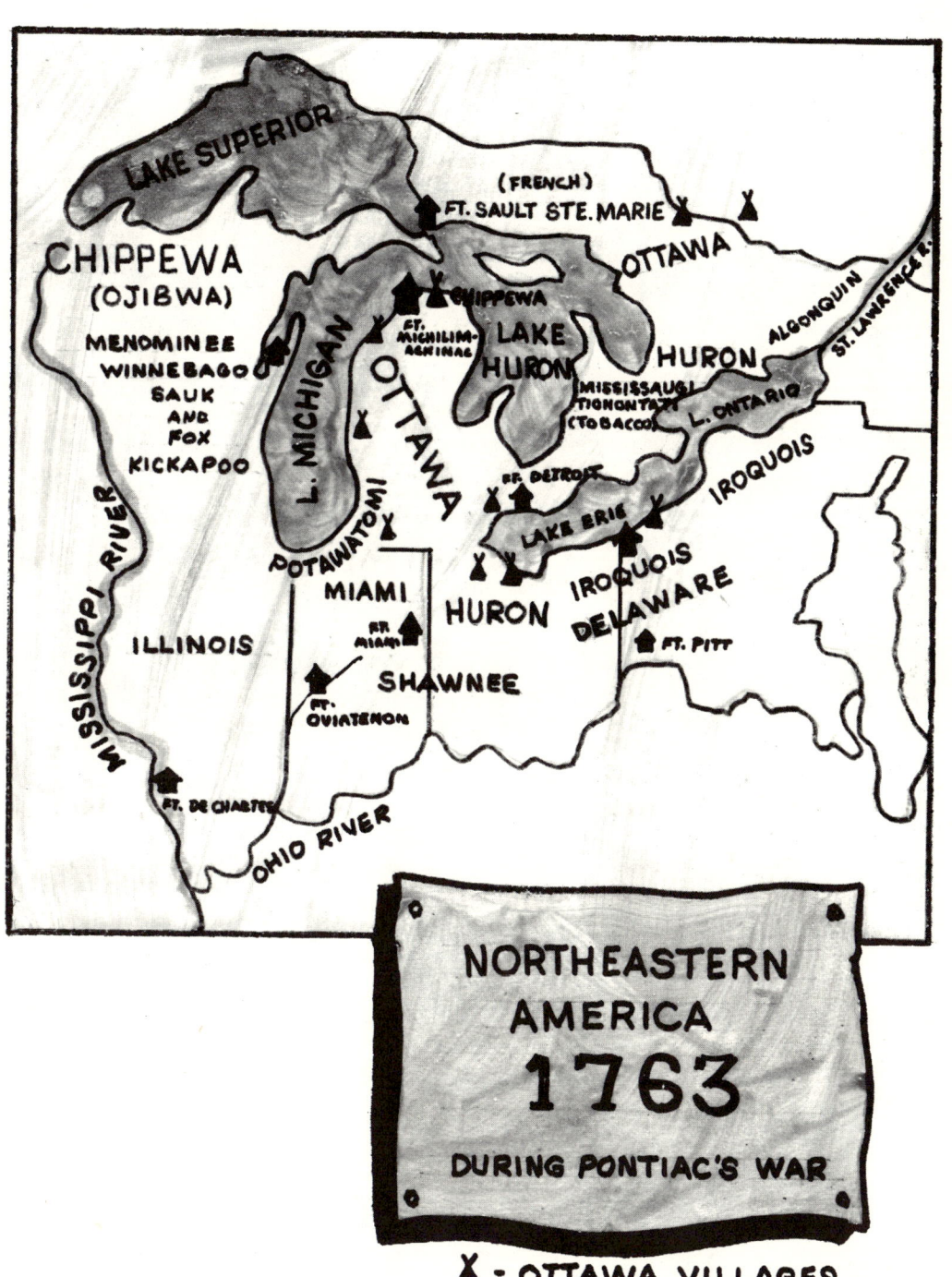

THE GREAT LAKES INDIANS

The first white men to live around the Great Lakes were French fur traders and missionaries. They found three large Indian tribes there — the Chippewa, the Potawatomi, and the Ottawa. All were allies.

Of the three tribes, the Ottawa were least friendly to the whites. They refused to become Christians, and they mistrusted the strangers.

Still, the Ottawa liked the French trade goods. They traded furs for guns, cloth, knives, needles, pots, and rum. They forgot their old way of life and came to depend on the things they obtained from the trading posts. They built their villages nearby.

About 1720, a boy named Pontiac was born in an unknown Ottawa village. Later he seems to have lived in a village near Fort

Detroit. His home was a hut called a wigwam, made of poles covered with bark.

Each spring, hundreds of Indians visited the fort and traded. The French were kind to them and there was peace among the tribes of the Great Lakes.

Young Pontiac grew tall and strong.

When he was about 16, Pontiac became a warrior. Each summer, the Ottawas and their allies went to war. They fought the Shawnees and Iroquois. These tribes had been moving westward as British settlers crowded them out of their old lands.

Pontiac became a famous war chief. Besides being brave, he was known as a great talker who could get people to do as he wanted.

In 1754, the French and British went to war to decide which would control the lands shown on the map. The Ottawa and other western tribes fought on the side of the French. Their customary way of making war was very cruel. The warriors killed not only soldiers, but also unarmed settlers, women, and children.

The British came to hate and fear all Indians — even friendly ones.

PONTIAC'S CONSPIRACY

The French and Indian War ended in 1760. The French lost. They had to move out of their forts and give up trading with the Indians. The British hurried to send their own soldiers to these forts.

At first, the British promised the Indians that everything would be better than before. But soon things were worse. British traders cheated the Indians. Settlers began to take Indian lands. The whites no longer gave them rum and gunpowder for their furs.

Two years passed. Pontiac grew more and more angry at what he felt were wrongs done to his people by the British. He began to plan a war.

His plan was truly amazing. He wanted all the tribes to forget their old quarrels and join together. Only if the red men fought together, he said, could they hope to defeat the British.

His plan was later called Pontiac's Conspiracy. He wanted the Indians to attack all of the British forts at one time. A war belt of red wampum was sent from Lake Ontario to the Mississippi River.

THE PONTIAC WAR BEGINS

On May 7, 1763, Pontiac began his war against the British. He led a large band of men into Fort Detroit. They had hidden guns. But someone had warned the British. The Indians had to retreat.

Pontiac was furious. He could not take the fort by surprise, so he attacked the British settlers outside. Then his army surrounded Fort Detroit and lay siege to it.

Pontiac did not harm the French people who still lived nearby. He told them: "We will drive the British away. Then we will give the fort back to you. It will be as it was before, in the good days."

Fort Detroit held fast. So Pontiac sent out bands to attack the other forts. Fort Sandusky fell to the Hurons. Men from Pontiac's own army took Fort Saint Joseph, Fort Miamis, and Fort Ouiatenon.

Far to the north, a band of Chippewas entered Fort Michilimackinac. They pretended to play a game of lacrosse. Then suddenly they attacked the soldiers and took the fort.

The British had only one western fort left — Fort Edward Augustus, at Green Bay. There were no troops to help them in case of attack, so the men there were ordered to surrender. They gave themselves up to friendly Indians.

Now the eastern tribes began to arise. Delawares attacked farms around Fort Pitt. Many people were killed. Others fled to the fort.

Senecas of the Iroquois Nation burned Fort Venango. They chased a small British force out of Fort LeBoeuf. Then an army of Senecas and Ottawas took Fort Presque Isle.

The war was only six weeks old, yet the Indians had already seized nine forts. Two others, Detroit and Pitt, were in grave danger. The British could hardly believe Pontiac had done it.

Meanwhile, Pontiac himself tried in vain to take Fort Detroit. Two British ships sailed up the Detroit River to bombard Pontiac's camp. He sent fire rafts against them, but the ships escaped.

Then fresh British troops arrived. Pontiac led a bloody battle that defeated them — but Fort Detroit itself still held. Pontiac hoped that the French would send help. He waited in vain.

THE UPRISING FAILS

Relief troops came to the people holding out at Fort Pitt. The Indians there had to retreat in August. But Pontiac still had Fort Detroit at bay and waited for the French to join him.

Late in October, a French officer brought a letter to Pontiac. The French and British had signed the Treaty of Paris and made peace.

Pontiac had no choice but to give up. Many of his Indian allies were tired of fighting. Winter was coming. They had to go back to their families.

The British tried to capture Pontiac. But he went to Illinois, to talk to the French.

The great conspiracy was over. Pontiac tried to stir up the Illinois Indians against the British, but news of his failure followed him from the East. The French commander at Fort de Chartres refused to help him. The fort was occupied by the British in 1765. Pontiac admitted defeat at last and helped the British subdue the last scattered bands of Indian fighters.

The great war chief was now a lonely exile in Illinois. Indians who had once followed him now hated him for giving up. In 1769, the Peoria tribe sent a brave to kill him. He

died of a stab in the back in Cahokia, Illinois. His war had started a fire of hatred between white men and red that would burn for more than 100 years — until the last western Indian surrendered to the white invaders.

GALLERY OF GREAT AMERICANS SERIES

INDIANS OF AMERICA
- GERONIMO
- CRAZY HORSE
- CHIEF JOSEPH
- PONTIAC
- SQUANTO
- OSCEOLA

EXPLORERS OF AMERICA
- COLUMBUS
- LEIF ERICKSEN
- DeSOTO
- LEWIS AND CLARK
- CHAMPLAIN
- CORONADO

FRONTIERSMEN OF AMERICA
- DANIEL BOONE
- BUFFALO BILL
- JIM BRIDGER
- FRANCIS MARION
- DAVY CROCKET
- KIT CARSON

WAR HEROES OF AMERICA
- JOHN PAUL JONES
- PAUL REVERE
- ROBERT E. LEE
- ULYSSES S. GRANT
- SAM HOUSTON
- LAFAYETTE

WOMEN OF AMERICA
- CLARA BARTON
- JANE ADAMS
- ELIZABETH BLACKWELL
- HARRIET TUBMAN
- SUSAN B. ANTHONY
- DOLLY MADISON

Imperial Public Library
Imperial, Texas